THE POCKET BOOK OF
Gratitude

UNLEASHING THE POWER OF THANKFULNESS
A 30 DAY GUIDE

JAY SHARPE

© 2017 Divine Works Publishing
ALL RIGHTS RESERVED

All rights reserved. No part of this publication may be reproduced, stored in a retrieval system, or transmitted in any form or by any means, electronic, mechanical, photocopying, recording or otherwise without the prior permission of the publisher or in accordance with the provisions of the Copyright, Designs, and Patents Act 1988 or under the terms of any license permitting limited copying issued by the Copyright Licensing Agency.

ISBN-13: 978-0-9996047-5-5

Published by:
Divine Works Publishing
Royal Palm Beach, Florida USA
www.divineworkspublishing.com
561-990-BOOK (2665)

Dedication

To the WOWman who raised me to be the WOWman I am today. She was the first person to tell me she enjoyed the letters I wrote her while she was abroad.
My strength, my inspiration, my rock.
My mom Sylvia Sharpe.

You get a WOW! -Woman of Worth.

My heart is filled with GRATITUDE for the love, patience, humility, and dedication you gave to all your children.

"Thank You Mommy. I love you."

Table of Contents

Foreword   *ix*
Acknowledgments   *xi*
Introduction   *xv*

Chapter One   *1*
   Gratitude is a Mindset
Chapter Two   *23*
   Expressing Physical Gratitude
Chapter Three   *45*
   Voicing Spiritual Gratitude
Closing Words   *75*
I've Lost Somethings in Life

About the Author   *93*

Foreword

Be grateful for the small things as well as the big things because that is the foundation of an abundant life. In *The Pocket Book of Gratitude,* Jay Sharpe teaches us that being thankful is the first step in the act of gratitude. We are constantly working on self-improvement and being grateful creates a pillar of strength as we move forward daily. She teaches that we should be grateful for the big things as well as the little things and to always be conscious of our state of gratefulness. This book is a fantastic read with tools to help us assess our lives daily to yield the highest and best benefit. Through faith and always being grateful despite dire circumstances, the spirit can still soar to achieve an abundant life.

The Pocketbook of Gratitude reveals how we each have the ability to secure and enjoy God's bounty as we determine to express gratefulness in our lives. The Questions and Answers sections gives each reader a chance to dig deep and find their own treasure trove of things to be grateful for and in turn build up their own tower of strength to deal with the adversities of life, while celebrating the amazing and wonderful things to be grateful for—both big and small. Enjoy your pursuit of an abundant life knowing that *"Gratitude conquers all!!"* This book is a gem and gives you the tools you need to experience the greater things that life has to offer.

-Attorney Eula R. Clarke

Acknowledgments

To my Triple C's: Chloe', Creed, & Cidney I am so grateful to be your mom. I appreciate your patience and your understanding for my laser focused attention while writing this book. I love you all so much. My prayer is that you will always be grateful for all of life's ups & downs. Remembering each crisis will always be either a blessing or a lesson.

Speak kindly, love deeply, help others, and always be true to yourself. With all my love and thankfulness unleashed.... Your Mom~

Thank you to:
Eula Clarke for always being there for my children, in my absence, as I completed this book.

My Publisher, Dr. Belinda John, for her sound advice and tireless efforts to capture my vision.

'Blinky' for joining the team of 'cheerleaders' and your generosity. My heart is full of gratitude.

My sister-friends.... Just WOW! All Women of Worth.

A special signal of gratitude to my daddy in heaven. Thank you for still being here in spirit.

#GratefulHeart

Endorsement

By Gary Cooper
Author of the book, *Shadow Dancing*

Jay Sharpe is one of the strongest women that I know, I feel honored to have witnessed one of the most traumatic times in her life (don't know how she did it), but the beauty of being around a person during a crisis is that you get a chance to see who they really are. She reminded me of my father's wise words *"tough challenges either make you into who you are not or into who you really are"* and in Jay's case, who better to speak to our spirits regarding gratitude than this powerful woman? In the face of conflict, *The Pocket Book of Gratitude* will help you realize your blessings.

Introduction

There's a secret weapon to abundant living and it's called GRATITUDE. In every area of your life, there is something to be thankful for. Gratitude changes everything, even in the most difficult situations. Gratitude unlocks the stagnation in your life and give you reasons to hope. There is no higher frequency to shift you to attracting better things in your life than gratitude. Gratitude elevates your consciousness to a state of positivity. Being appreciative should be a lifestyle not just a 'sometime event.' If you want to see positive results manifest in your life, practice daily acts of gratefulness. Be thankful for everything and anything. Sit in a place of thankfulness. Say "thank you" for the big things as well as the small things. *"I am grateful for"* should be a verbal declaration in your daily living.

My hope is that this book will help you to create a lifestyle of appreciation. With each daily practice, you will see and feel the energy of gratitude. You will experience less stress in your life as you move through the workbook. Read your gratitude statements. Speak out loud your affirmations. Learn a methodical fact in life and list the things you are grateful for. There are more things in your life to be thankful for than you think.

During a very difficult time in my life, caused by a heart-breaking tragedy, (my home was destroyed by fire on New Year's Day.) I set the intention to write a gratitude statement each day that I felt burdened down. Through this process, I discovered that by practicing thankfulness, I focused less on negative things, which allowed me to focus more on positive ones. I began to even appreciate the unpleasant feelings and thoughts that would arise during that period. Most of my days were spent focusing on the people, places and things I was thankful for. I eventually became mentally, physically, and spiritually stronger.

The exercises in this book will help you to discover that there are so many things to be thankful for. I invite you to set the intention to start and complete this process regardless of what is happening around you or to you. Be committed to allowing yourself the opportunity to feel good about life. You are life! Give yourself permission to move through this process without the expectation of a specific result. Instead allow the process to guide your mind, body, and spirit to a state of abundance by being grateful.

Dr. Maya Angelou is my all-time favorite author. Her quotes of gratitude helped me to shift my thoughts to practicing gratitude in my daily affirmations. Here are three of my favorite teachings from her.

"Let gratitude be the pillow on which you kneel to say your nightly prayer."

"When you have an attitude of gratitude you wake up saying thank you."

"There's nothing greater you can say to God, than thank you."

The more grateful you are, the better things you will attract. Start and end each day with gratitude.

Chapter One

GRATITUDE IS A MINDSET

The mind is powerful.
Use it wisely and it will reward you immensely.
When the mind sits in a state of gratitude the possibilities are endless. Gratitude is a required mindset for living an abundant lifestyle.

Day One

Gratitude Statement: *"I love being a <u>Woman</u>. I am thankful for the inspiration of other strong, amazing, and brilliant women."*

Affirmation Statement: (Say it out loud) *"I appreciate and respect my gender."*

Fact: The two highest IQ scores recorded in history belong to women.

Exercise: List the names of three women in your life (past or present) who you are thankful for and why.

1: _____
_____
_____
_____
_____

2: _____
_____
_____
_____
_____

3: _____
_____
_____
_____
_____

CHAPTER ONE — GRATITUDE IS A MINDSET

*It's important that you love who you are created to be.
Women are one of the greatest gifts to humanity.*

*You are a vessel full of power with
a hidden treasure on the inside of you.*

*It is imperative for your soul's evolution that you
acknowledge the women in your life who
have inspired you.*

*Think about the reasons you
appreciate the role they
play in your life.*

Grateful Heart

Day Two

Gratitude Statement: *"Today I am grateful for my <u>Parent/Parents</u>. I am thankful that they made the choice to raise and guide me."*

Affirmation Statement: (Say it out loud) *"I appreciate my parents for raising me."*

Fact: There are about 85 million mothers in America, according to a recent U.S. Census Bureau estimate.

Exercise: List three things you are thankful to your parents/parent for and why.

1: _____
_____
_____
_____

2: _____
_____
_____
_____

3: _____
_____
_____
_____

CHAPTER ONE — GRATITUDE IS A MINDSET

Parenting is not for the faint of heart.

Parenting requires skills, patience, and a whole lot of love~

Grateful Heart

Day Three

Gratitude Statement: *"Today I am grateful for my Family and Friends around the world. I am thankful for their love, laughter, and light."*

Affirmation Statement: (Say it out loud) *"I accept my family and friends for who they are."*

Fact: As of 2014, most families are made up of step-families, singles and families living together outside of marriage.

Exercise: List the names of three friends or family members who you are thankful for and why.

1: _____
_____
_____
_____
_____

2: _____
_____
_____
_____
_____

3: _____
_____
_____
_____
_____

Family and friends give you a sense of familiarity and belonging.

You feel safe and loved when you are around them~

Grateful Heart

Day Four

Gratitude Statement: *"Today I am grateful for the ability to <u>Inspire, Impact, and Influence</u> others in a positive way."*

Affirmation Statement: (Say it out loud) *"I am a giver of love, appreciation, and compassion."*

Fact: 'It is critical to note that people who've made a real difference aren't all privileged, advantaged or "special" by any stretch. Many come from disadvantaged families, crushing circumstances, and in limited capabilities, but have found ways to pick themselves up and rise above their circumstances (and their genes) to transform their own lives and those around them.' (Kathy Caprino)

Exercise: List three ways in which you have made a positive impression on someone's life and how that makes you feel.

1: _____
_____
_____
_____

2: _____
_____
_____
_____

3: _____
_____
_____
_____

CHAPTER ONE — GRATITUDE IS A MINDSET

*You are more powerful
than you think~*

Grateful Heart

Day Five

Gratitude Statement: *"Today I am grateful for <u>Life</u>. There have been times where I could have been lost, but my Creator and Source sustained me. I am so thankful"*

Affirmation Statement: (Say it out loud) *"I accept me, just as I am."*

Fact: Life is the consciousness of humanity. It is the perception of the world and the universe. (Philosophynow.org) The average person walks 75,000 miles (120,000 KM) in a lifetime or five times round the world. An average person spends 6 years of his life dreaming.

Exercise: List three things about your life that you are thankful for and why.

1: _____
_____
_____

2: _____
_____
_____

3: _____
_____
_____

CHAPTER ONE — GRATITUDE IS A MINDSET

Life is a gift.

You are Life ~

Grateful Heart

Day Six

Gratitude Statement: *"Today I am grateful for <u>Music</u>. Music soothes my soul and eases my pain."*

Affirmation Statement: (Say it out loud) *"I appreciate and enjoy music."*

Fact: Scientists ran experiments by monitoring brain activity and found that music caused dopamine peaks and emotional arousal. This release of dopamine is connected to why people place such a high emphasis on music's ability to manipulate our emotions. Music can quite literally alter the chemical balances in your brain.

Exercise: List three songs which help you cope through difficult times in your life.

1: _____
_____
_____
_____

2: _____
_____
_____
_____

3: _____
_____
_____
_____

CHAPTER ONE — GRATITUDE IS A MINDSET

*"One good thing about music,
when it hits you feel no pain."
-Bob Marley*

Grateful Heart

Day Seven

Gratitude Statement: *"Today I am grateful for <u>Wisdom</u>. It's not enough for me to just know, it's more important for me to know my WHY..."*

Affirmation Statement: (Say it out loud) *"I deal with life experiences with wisdom and understanding."*

Fact: Between the age of 17-25 years is referred to as the 'Age of Wisdom.'

Exercise: List three wise statements that you are grateful for.

1: _____
_____
_____
_____
_____

2: _____
_____
_____
_____
_____

3: _____
_____
_____
_____
_____

*Knowledge is Essential
and
Wisdom is Paramount ~*

Grateful Heart

Day Eight

Gratitude Statement: *"Today I am grateful for <u>Community</u>. A community that supports each other will always thrive. It is important to 'give back' to my community in which I reside. Volunteering is a great way to 'give back' and to be of service to others."*

Affirmation Statement: (Say it out loud) *"I enjoy supporting my community with my gifts and talents."*

Fact: People who have a community in their lives feel more valued and important.

Exercise: List three organizations in your community that you are involved in or grateful for.

1: _____
_____
_____
_____
_____

2: _____
_____
_____
_____
_____

3: _____
_____
_____
_____
_____

CHAPTER ONE — GRATITUDE IS A MINDSET

*We are all here to be of service
to others in a positive way ~*

Grateful Heart

Day Nine

Gratitude Statement: *"Today I am grateful for <u>Serenity</u>. Serenity brings peace and comfort in difficult times. It's important for me to create a physical space in my home, where I can sit, reflect, and meditate."*

Affirmation Statement: (Say it out loud) *"I bring serenity into my space each day."*

Fact: The word serenity comes from the Latin serenus, meaning clear or unclouded (skies).

Exercise: List three places where you can find serenity and express gratitude.

1: _____
_____
_____
_____
_____

2: _____
_____
_____
_____
_____

3: _____
_____
_____
_____
_____

Be grateful for tranquility.

Serenity is bliss.

Listen to serenity ~

Grateful Heart

Day Ten

Gratitude Statement: *"Today I am grateful for <u>Thoughts</u>. I am mindful of the thoughts I harbor. I control my thoughts by applying positive thinking."*

Affirmation Statement: (Say it out loud) *"I intentionally dismiss negative thoughts from my mind as they arise."*

Fact: Scientific research shows that a person has over 50,000 thoughts per day. This means 1,000-5,000 per minute.

Exercise: List three positive thoughts that you are having right now.

1: _____
_____
_____
_____

2: _____
_____
_____
_____

3: _____
_____
_____
_____

CHAPTER ONE — GRATITUDE IS A MINDSET

Think Positive Thoughts ~

Grateful Heart

Chapter Two

EXPRESSING PHYSICAL GRATITUDE

Physical health is critical for overall well-being and is the most visible of the various dimensions of health, which also include social, intellectual, emotional, spiritual and environmental health.

(Study.com/academy)

Day One

Gratitude Statement: *"Today I am grateful for <u>Health</u>. When I take care of my body I can cope better during a difficult time. I need to be healthy to heal."*

Affirmation Statement: (Say it out loud) *"My health is the most important thing to me."*

Fact: Health is wealth.

Exercise: List two healthy habits in which you take care of yourself and one healthy food that you consume for maintaining your health.

1: _____
_____
_____
_____
_____

2: _____
_____
_____
_____
_____

3: _____
_____
_____
_____
_____

CHAPTER TWO – EXPRESSING PHYSICAL GRATITUDE

Health is Wealth ~

Grateful Heart

Day Two

Gratitude Statement: *"Today I am grateful for <u>Strength</u>. Physical strength is essential to healing. It allows my body to sustain the pain of grief, loss, or trauma. Exercise is key to maintaining physical strength."*

Affirmation Statement: (Say it out loud) *"I am stronger than I think."*

Fact: 60% of people who weight train get an average of 7 hours or more of sleep per night.

Exercise: List three workouts that you enjoy doing and the area of your body that it strengthens.

1: _____
_____
_____
_____
_____

2: _____
_____
_____
_____
_____

3: _____
_____
_____
_____
_____

CHAPTER TWO — EXPRESSING PHYSICAL GRATITUDE

*Don't quit!
You are already in pain.
You already hurt.
Get a reward from it ~*

Grateful Heart

Day Three

Gratitude Statement: *"Today I am grateful for <u>Rest</u>. Rest is important for my health. My body needs rest. I give myself permission to relax, rejuvenate and rest. When I am tired my body cannot be productive. I take the time to unwind and rest."*

Affirmation Statement: (Say it out loud) *"I give my body permission to rest."*

Fact: Getting good sleep protects overall health and keeps things like memory functioning normally.

Exercise: List three ways in which you can relax and get some rest.

1: _____
_____
_____
_____

2: _____
_____
_____
_____

3: _____
_____
_____
_____

CHAPTER TWO — EXPRESSING PHYSICAL GRATITUDE

*"Six days you shall work,
but on the seventh day you must rest"
(Exodus 34:21)*

Grateful Heart

Day Four

Gratitude Statement: *"Today I am grateful for my <u>Physical Appearance</u>. I appreciate the way I look. I am thankful for my physical attributes. I am created in the image of my Creator. I am unique. I am beautiful. No one compares to me."*

Affirmation Statement: (Say it out loud) *"I am perfect just as I am."*

Fact: There's a lot a person will assume about you based on your physical appearance.

Exercise: List three physical features about your appearance that you are thankful for.

1: _____
_____
_____
_____

2: _____
_____
_____
_____

3: _____
_____
_____
_____

CHAPTER TWO — EXPRESSING PHYSICAL GRATITUDE

You are uniquely and wonderfully made ~

Grateful Heart

Day Five

Gratitude Statement: *"Today I am grateful for my <u>DNA</u>. My DNA links me to my ancestry. It carries my genetic information."*

Affirmation Statement: (Say it out loud) *"Greatness is in my DNA!"*

Fact: DNA is built using only four building blocks, the nucleotides adenine, guanine, thymine, and cytosine. DNA stands for deoxyribonucleic acid.

Exercise: List three relatives and what similar features or traits you share with them.

1: _____
_____
_____
_____

2: _____
_____
_____
_____

3: _____
_____
_____
_____

Did you know that your DNA determines your eye color, hair color and even the size of your nose?

Grateful Heart

Day Six

Gratitude Statement: *"Today I am grateful for <u>Sight</u>. I take care of my eyesight. My eyes are the windows to my soul. The ability to see is a gift denied to many. I can see with a vision in mind."*

Affirmation Statement: (Say it out loud) *"I love the ability to see all the beauty surrounding me."*

Fact: The average blink lasts for about 1/10th of a second.

Exercise: List two ways in which you take care of your eyesight and list one vision you have for your life.

1: _____
_____
_____
_____

2: _____
_____
_____
_____

3: _____
_____
_____
_____

CHAPTER TWO — EXPRESSING PHYSICAL GRATITUDE

*"It's a terrible thing to see
and have no vision."
-Helen Keller*

Grateful Heart

Day Seven

Gratitude Statement: *"Today I am grateful for my* <u>Hands.</u> *My hands carry my authentic qualities. When I look at the palm of my hands I see the lines drawn. They tell a story. When I look at my fingers the way they are shaped, they hold my specific print. No one else has my fingerprint. I give thanks for my hands. I use them to create and help others. *Clap your hands and hold them up in the air and praise God for your hands."*

Affirmation Statement: (Say it out loud) *"I enjoy lending a hand."*

Fact: The palm of your hand does not have the ability to tan.

Exercise: List three qualities about your hands that you appreciate and why.

1: _____
_____
_____
_____

2: _____
_____
_____
_____

3: _____
_____
_____
_____

CHAPTER TWO — EXPRESSING PHYSICAL GRATITUDE

*You have two hands.
One to help yourself and
one to help others~*

Grateful Heart

Day Eight

Gratitude Statement: *"Today I am grateful for my <u>Body</u>. I love the shape of my body. I love the curves, lines, and the contour of my body. I am thankful that I have a body to experience my life journey."*

Affirmation Statement: (Say it out loud) *"My body is the temple for the Holy Spirit."*

Fact: An adult human being is made up of around 7,000,000,000,000,000,000,000,000,000 atoms.

Exercise: List three features of your body that you appreciate.

1: _____
_____
_____
_____

2: _____
_____
_____
_____

3: _____
_____
_____
_____

*Your body is a vessel full
of unlimited power ~*

Grateful Heart

Day Nine

Gratitude Statement: *"Today I am grateful for my <u>Voice.</u> I use my voice to sing. I use my voice to speak. I use my voice to express my thoughts. My voice is unique. It can make a variation of sounds. My voice has a distinct pitch, tone and cadence."*

Affirmation Statement: (Say it out loud) *"I use my voice to speak truth and love."*

Fact: The most complex language to voice is Xóõ, spoken mostly in Botswana. It has 112 distinct sounds. English, by comparison, has about 40.

Exercise: List three unique qualities about your voice.

1: _____
_____
_____
_____
_____

2: _____
_____
_____
_____
_____

3: _____
_____
_____
_____
_____

Use your voice to speak life~

Grateful Heart

Day Ten

Gratitude Statement: *"Today I am grateful for my <u>Heart</u>. I love my heart with all my heart. This is a place where love resides. I love to feel the beating of my heart against my chest. I love to hear a baby's heartbeat. I listen to the rhythm of my heartbeat when I am meditating. My heart is made for love."*

Affirmation Statement: (Say it out loud) *"My heart is made for love."*

Fact: Your heart is one giant pump. Every minute, your heart pumps about five quarts of blood through a system of blood vessels that's over 60,000 miles long, according to the Cleveland Clinic. That translates to about 2,000 gallons of blood every day.

Exercise: Name three things that you love about your heart.

1: _____
_____
_____
_____

2: _____
_____
_____
_____

3: _____
_____
_____
_____

CHAPTER TWO — EXPRESSING PHYSICAL GRATITUDE

Love with all your heart~

Grateful Heart

43

Chapter Three

VOICING SPIRITUAL GRATITUDE

*I believe in the power of the human spirit.
It guides us in a divine way. There's an abundance of
wealth that lies within the human spirit.
It teaches us how to be and become.*

Day One

Gratitude Statement: *"Today I am grateful for <u>Blessings.</u> Blessings are divine gifts. Blessings comes to me in abundance. I am thankful for the abundance of blessings I have received throughout my life journey."*

Affirmation Statement: (Say it out loud) *"I am blessed to be a blessing to others."*

Fact: Blessing is a two-way movement of (from humans to God) thanksgiving and praise, and of (from God to humans) power and good fortune.

Exercise: List three ways in which you have experienced divine blessings.

1: _____
_____
_____
_____

2: _____
_____
_____
_____

3: _____
_____
_____
_____

CHAPTER THREE — VOICING SPIRITUAL GRATITUDE

I am Blessed~

Grateful Heart

Day Two

Gratitude Statement: *"Today I am grateful for Prayer. My prayer is an appeal to God. My prayer is a vital part of my day. My prayer honors God. My prayer is an invocation to something larger than myself. My prayer keeps me grounded in the sovereignty of God."*

Affirmation Statement: (Say it out loud) *"Prayer is my communication with God."*

Fact: May 5th is the National Day of Prayer in the United States of America.

Exercise: List three areas of your life that you need to pray about.

1: _____
_____
_____
_____
_____

2: _____
_____
_____
_____
_____

3: _____
_____
_____
_____
_____

CHAPTER THREE – VOICING SPIRITUAL GRATITUDE

P.U.S.H
Pray Until Something Happens ~

Grateful Heart

Day Three

Gratitude Statement: *"Today I am grateful for <u>Meditation</u>. The act of meditation is amazing! Meditation helps me to center my thoughts and allows the spirit of God to navigate through my body. I feel a deeper connection to my creator when I meditate."*

Affirmation Statement: (Say it out loud) *"I meditate to hear from God."*

Fact: Meditation is a way to reduce stress by focusing your attention and eliminating the stream of jumbled thoughts that may be crowding your mind.

Exercise: List three ways in which you practice meditation.

1: _____
_____
_____
_____

2:_____
_____
_____
_____

3:_____
_____
_____
_____

Meditate to appreciate ~

Grateful Heart

Day Four

Gratitude Statement: *"Today I am grateful for <u>Stillness</u>. There's richness in stillness. I will be still and listen to the voice within. I appreciate this statement because it reminds me to be still and know that my creator is God."*

Affirmation Statement: (Say it out loud) *"Stillness gives me a place of comfort."*

Fact: Stillness is the absence of motion.

Exercise: List three ways in which you practice being still.

1: _____
_____
_____

2: _____
_____
_____

3: _____
_____
_____

"Be still and know that I am God"
        -Psalm 46;10

Grateful Heart

Day Five

Gratitude Statement: *"Today I am grateful for <u>Praise & Worship.</u> 'I will enter into His gates with thanksgiving and into His courts with praise' and do so with gladness of heart."*

Affirmation Statement: (Say it out loud) *"Let every breath and all that I am never cease to worship you oh Lord."*

Fact: The word proskuneo "to worship" means to bow down to God.

Exercise: List three ways in which you worship and give thanks to God.

1: _____
_____
_____
_____

2: _____
_____
_____
_____
_____

3: _____
_____
_____
_____
_____

CHAPTER THREE – VOICING SPIRITUAL GRATITUDE

It's my joy to worship you God ~

Grateful Heart

Day Six

Gratitude Statement: *"Today I am grateful for <u>Hope</u>. The hope in me is greater than the lack. I have great expectations for my life. I live in a place of hope. There's a miracle in hope. Hope fuels the engine of my faith. It gives me the willingness to keep moving forward. There are things that I hope for. I hope that one day this world will be ruled only by love."*

Affirmation Statement: (Say it out loud) *"I choose to find hope in difficult times."*

Fact: Hope is an optimistic state of mind, where regardless of your circumstances, you expect a positive outcome.

Exercise: What three things are you hopeful for today?

1: _____
_____
_____
_____

2: _____
_____
_____
_____

3: _____
_____
_____
_____

*Don't lose hope,
you never know what
tomorrow may bring ~*

Grateful Heart

Day Seven

Gratitude Statement: *"Today I am grateful for <u>Trust</u>. I trust in God. I trust He will always provide, protect, and preserve me. I have good relationships that are built on trust; knowing that the other person has my back. God promised to never leave or forsake me. I trust that promise."*

Affirmation Statement: (Say it out loud) *"I am trustworthy and deserve to be trusted."*

Fact: Trust is a bond formed by two or more entities.

Exercise: List three ways in which you show trust.

1: _____
_____
_____
_____

2: _____
_____
_____
_____

3: _____
_____
_____
_____

CHAPTER THREE — VOICING SPIRITUAL GRATITUDE

I Trust You Lord ~

Grateful Heart

Day Eight

Gratitude Statement: *"Today I am grateful for <u>Grace.</u> We are living in the age of Grace. God's grace is sufficient for me. I am grateful for the abundance of divine favor in my life."*

Affirmation Statement: (Say it out loud) *"God's grace is a blessing to me each day."*

Fact: The word grace comes from the Latin word 'gratia' which means God's favor.

Exercise: List three ways in which you exercise grace.

1: _____
_____
_____
_____
_____

2: _____
_____
_____
_____
_____

3: _____
_____
_____
_____
_____

CHAPTER THREE — VOICING SPIRITUAL GRATITUDE

*Grace carried me here
and grace will carry me on ~*

Grateful Heart

Day Nine

Gratitude Statement: *"Today I am grateful for <u>Belief</u>. I am a believer. I believe in God. I believe in the power of my creator. I believe there is more good than bad. I believe in kindness, love, peace……. I believe!"*

Affirmation Statement: (Say it out loud) *"I believe in me."*

Fact: A belief is a conviction based on cultural or personal faith, morality, or values.

Exercise: Write three of your belief statements below.

1: _____
_____
_____
_____

2: _____
_____
_____
_____

3: _____
_____
_____
_____

*Believe in yourself and
you will be unstoppable~*

Grateful Heart

Day Ten

Gratitude Statement: *"Today I am grateful for <u>Love.</u> There is no power on earth stronger than love. Love makes all things possible. Love is patient, love is kind. It does not envy, it does not boast, it is not proud. It does not dishonor others, it is not self-seeking, it is not easily angered, it keeps no record of wrongs. Love does not delight in evil but rejoices with the truth. It always protects, always trusts, always hopes, always perseveres. Love never fails."*

Affirmation Statement: (Say it out loud) *"I believe in love and all its possibilities."*

Fact: Love has similar neurological effects as a cocaine high. In both cases, the brain is flooded by an excess of dopamine. The more dopamine that floods the brain, the more "high" you feel. This is the exact same process that accompanies a cocaine high.

Exercise: List three ways in which you express love.

1: _____
_____
_____

2: _____
_____
_____

3: _____
_____
_____

CHAPTER THREE — VOICING SPIRITUAL GRATITUDE

Love is all things possible~

Grateful Heart

*Gratitude is the alchemy of Faith,
Hope & Love. It is a magical process of
transformation and creation combined.
It can be subtle or it can be bold.
It includes the perfectly blended
harmony of self love, acceptance,
and worth.*

*Gratitude is not an action word,
it is an active energy, transmitting
waves of ebb and flow.*

SOURCES CITED:
FACTS reference links

The two highest IQ scores recorded in history belongs to women.
https://en.wikipedia.org/wiki/Marilyn_vos_Savant

There are about 85 million mothers in America, according to a recent U.S. Census Bureau estimate.
www.pewresearch.org/fact.../5-questions-and-answers-about-american-moms-today/

As of 2014, most families are made up of stepfamilies, singles and families living together outside of marriage.
https://www.huffingtonpost.com/mary-t.../3-surprising-facts-about-_b_6543440.html

'It's critical to note that people who've made a real difference aren't all privileged, advantaged or "special" by any stretch. Many come from disadvantaged families, crushing circumstances and initially limited capabilities, but have found ways to pick themselves up and rise above their circumstances (and their genes) to transform their own lives and those around them.'
https://www.taigacompany.com/leadership-qualities-changing-the-world-for-the-better/

Life is the consciousness of humanity. It is the perception of the world and the universe.
https://philosophynow.org/issues/101/What_Is_Life
The average person walks 75,000 miles (120,000 KM) in a lifetime or five times round the world. An average person spends 6 years of his life dreaming
https://www.unbelievable-facts.com/2015/05/lifetime-facts.html/4

Scientists ran experiments by monitoring brain activity and found that music caused dopamine peaks and emotional arousal. This release of dopamine is connected to why people place such a high emphasis on music's ability to manipulate our emotions. Music can quite literally alter the chemical balances in your brain.
https://www.iorbitnews.com › Columns

Between the age of 17-25 years is referred to as the 'Age of Wisdom.' https://www.abcchildrensdentistry.com/edu_resources/wisdom-teeth/

People who have a community in their lives feel more valued and important. https://books.google.com/books?isbn=0231518021

The word serenity comes from the Latin serenus, meaning clear or unclouded (skies). https://www.blog.adw.org/2012/03/what-is-serenity-and-how-can-i-grow-in-it/

Scientific research shows that a person has over 50,000 thoughts per day. This means 1,000-5,000 per minute. https://subliminalpro.com/thoughts/

60% of people who weight train get an average of 7 hours or more of sleep per night. https://www.sfhp.ehe.osu.edu/strength-training/

DNA is built using only four building blocks, the nucleotides adenine, guanine, thymine, and cytosine. DNA stands for deoxyribonucleic acid. https://www.genome.gov/25520880/Deoxyribonucleic-Acid-DNA-Fact-Sheet

The average blink lasts for about 1/10th of a second. https://www.pinterest.com/pin/528750812472478297/

An adult human being is made up of around 7,000,000,000,000,000,000,000,000,000 atoms. https://www.theguardian.com/science/2013/jan/27/20-human-body-facts-science

The most complex language to voice is! Xóõ, spoken mostly in Botswana. It has 112 distinct sounds. English, by comparison, has about 40 https://www.discovermagazine.com/2015/sept/20-things-human-voice

Your heart is one giant pump. Every minute, your heart pumps about five quarts of blood through a system of blood vessels that's over 60,000 miles long, according to the Cleveland Clinic. That translates to about 2,000 gallons of blood every day. https://www.arheart.com › Heart Health

Meditation is a way to reduce stress by focusing your attention and eliminating the stream of jumbled thoughts that may be crowding your mind.
https://uhs.berkeley.edu/.../article_-_meditation_a_simple_fast_way_to_reduce_stress....

The word proskuneo "to worship" means to bow down to God.
https://www.studylight.org/language-studies/greek-thoughts.html?article=80

The word grace comes from the Latin word 'gratia' which means God's favor.' *www.ficotw.org/grace.html*

Fact: Love has similar neurological effects as a cocaine high. In both cases, the brain is flooded by an excess of dopamine. The more dopamine that floods the brain, the more "high" you feel. This is the exact same process that accompanies a cocaine high.
https://www.buzzfeed.com/regajha/heartwarming-facts-about-love

Psalm 23

The Lord is my shepherd; I shall not want.

He maketh me to lie down in green pastures: he leadeth me beside the still waters.

He restoreth my soul: he leadeth me in the paths of righteousness for his name's sake.

Yea, though I walk through the valley of the shadow of death, I will fear no evil: for thou art with me; thy rod and thy staff they comfort me.

Thou preparest a table before me in the presence of mine enemies: thou anointest my head with oil; my cup runneth over.

Surely goodness and mercy shall follow me all the days of my life: and I will dwell in the house of the Lord for ever.

Amen.

I've Lost Somethings in Life

By: Jay Sharpe

I've lost some friendships.
I've lost my home.
I've lost some loved ones.
I've even lost my step.
I've lost my temper.
I've lost some opportunities.
I've lost some relationships.
I've lost some jobs.
I even lost my breath.
I've lost some possessions.
I've lost my courage.
I've lost some battles.
I've lost my strength.........
But there's one thing I have never lost.......
I have never lost my PRAISE!
Keep on, keeping on.

Through it all with GRATITUDE!

#gratefulheart ♥

About the Author

"The unthinkable happened on New Year's Day 2017. Our home was destroyed by a house fire at approximately 5am and my faith was shaken. 'How could this be?" I thought, as I struggled with the grief of this trauma. I found myself in a place of hopelessness, fear and worry. I couldn't comprehend the pain I was feeling and how much it affected me and my entire existence. I am known to be resilient, but I was feeling no such thing during that time. All I wanted to do was lay down somewhere... anywhere and call it the end. I pretty much wanted to die. I didn't see a way out of this, and my family was hurting, and I was hurting for them. I couldn't 'fix' this one. I couldn't make it 'better'... something I had grown accustom to doing for them. Day three after the fire, would cause me to entertain thoughts of suicide. Death seemed the best option as the dark 'smoke' of fear hovered over my head...."

Jay Sharpe, is a mother, effective Certified Professional Life & Grief Coach, well sought after dynamic speaker, Blog Talk Radio Show Host, Freelance Writer, and Author of the book *Chicken Lyrics - Book of Quotes*.

She is a strong advocate for young girls and women's empowerment, evolution, and harmonization. She uses her platform to Inspire, Impact & Influence them in positive ways. Her work has appeared in TCPalm newspaper, and Panache Magazine Jamaica.

Jay has developed several coaching tools and programs which she successfully uses in her workshops internationally. She is a board member of Molly's House Inc., a hospitality home that helps keeps families together during a medical crisis as well as a 2017/2018 nominee for the Women of Distinction—Soroptimist International of Stuart Florida.

Jay is a strong believer that Gratitude unlocks the door to abundant living.

To book Jay Sharpe to speak at your event:
email: coachjaysharpe.fire@gmail.com
www.jaysharpe.com

www.ingramcontent.com/pod-product-compliance
Lightning Source LLC
Chambersburg PA
CBHW050442010526
44118CB00013B/1643